50 Chocolate Cooking Recipes

By: Kelly Johnson

Table of Contents

- Classic Chocolate Cake
- Chocolate Chip Cookies
- Chocolate Mousse
- Chocolate Brownies
- Chocolate Truffles
- Chocolate Fudge
- Chocolate Lava Cake
- Chocolate Pudding
- Chocolate Tart
- Chocolate Cupcakes
- Chocolate Cheesecake
- Chocolate Ganache
- Chocolate Almond Bark
- Chocolate Ice Cream
- Chocolate Chip Muffins
- Chocolate Soufflé
- Chocolate Covered Strawberries

- Chocolate-Dipped Pretzels
- Chocolate Eclairs
- Chocolate Hazelnut Spread
- Chocolate Fondue
- Chocolate Milkshake
- Chocolate Chia Pudding
- Chocolate Peanut Butter Cups
- Hot Chocolate
- Chocolate Croissants
- Chocolate Coconut Balls
- Chocolate Popcorn
- Chocolate Banana Bread
- Chocolate Chip Pancakes
- Chocolate Caramel Brownies
- Chocolate Chip Scones
- Chocolate-Orange Truffles
- Chocolate-Covered Almonds
- Chocolate Dipped Marshmallows
- Chocolate Macarons

- Chocolate-Covered Pretzel Bites
- Chocolate Ricotta Pie
- Chocolate Toffee Bars
- Chocolate Rice Krispies Treats
- Chocolate Tiramisu
- Chocolate Coconut Macaroons
- Chocolate Cherry Cake
- Chocolate Ice Cream Sandwiches
- Chocolate Chip Cheesecake Bars
- Chocolate-Dipped Biscotti
- Chocolate Peanut Butter Brownies
- Chocolate Fudge Cake
- Chocolate Mint Cookies
- Chocolate Cinnamon Rolls

Classic Chocolate Cake
Ingredients:

- 1 ¾ cups flour
- 1 ½ cups sugar
- ¾ cup cocoa powder
- 1 ½ tsp baking powder
- 1 ½ tsp baking soda
- 1 tsp salt
- 2 eggs
- 1 cup milk
- ½ cup vegetable oil
- 2 tsp vanilla extract
- 1 cup boiling water

Instructions:
Preheat oven to 350°F (175°C).
Mix dry ingredients in one bowl and wet ingredients in another.
Combine both and mix until smooth.
Pour into greased cake pans and bake for 30-35 minutes.
Cool and frost with chocolate frosting.

Chocolate Chip Cookies
Ingredients:

- 2 ¼ cups flour
- 1 tsp baking soda
- ½ tsp salt
- 1 cup unsalted butter (softened)
- ¾ cup sugar
- ¾ cup brown sugar
- 2 tsp vanilla extract
- 2 eggs
- 2 cups chocolate chips

Instructions:
Preheat oven to 350°F (175°C).
Mix flour, baking soda, and salt in one bowl.
Cream together butter, sugars, and vanilla, then add eggs.
Gradually add the dry ingredients, then fold in chocolate chips.
Scoop dough onto a baking sheet and bake for 10-12 minutes.

Chocolate Mousse

Ingredients:

- 8 oz dark chocolate
- 1 cup heavy cream
- 2 tbsp sugar
- 1 tsp vanilla extract

Instructions:
Melt chocolate in a heatproof bowl over simmering water.
Whip the cream and sugar until soft peaks form.
Fold the whipped cream into the melted chocolate.
Chill in the fridge for at least 2 hours before serving.

Chocolate Brownies
Ingredients:

- 1 cup unsalted butter
- 1 cup sugar
- 1 cup brown sugar
- 4 large eggs
- 1 tsp vanilla extract
- 1 cup cocoa powder
- 1 ½ cups flour
- ½ tsp baking powder
- ¼ tsp salt

Instructions:
Preheat oven to 350°F (175°C).
Melt butter and mix with sugars.
Add eggs and vanilla, then stir in dry ingredients.
Pour batter into a greased pan and bake for 30-35 minutes.
Let cool before cutting into squares.

Chocolate Truffles

Ingredients:

- 8 oz dark chocolate
- ½ cup heavy cream
- 1 tbsp butter
- Cocoa powder or chopped nuts (for coating)

Instructions:
Melt chocolate, cream, and butter together.
Let cool, then refrigerate for 2 hours.
Once firm, scoop and roll into balls, then coat in cocoa powder or nuts.
Chill again before serving.

Chocolate Fudge
Ingredients:

- 2 cups chocolate chips
- 1 can (14 oz) sweetened condensed milk
- 1 tsp vanilla extract

Instructions:
Melt chocolate chips and sweetened condensed milk in a saucepan over low heat.
Once smooth, stir in vanilla.
Pour into a greased pan and let cool until firm, then cut into squares.

Chocolate Lava Cake
 Ingredients:

- 1 cup semi-sweet chocolate chips
- ½ cup unsalted butter
- 1 cup powdered sugar
- 2 eggs
- 2 egg yolks
- 1 tsp vanilla extract
- ¼ cup flour

Instructions:
Preheat oven to 425°F (220°C).
Melt chocolate and butter together.
Mix in powdered sugar, eggs, egg yolks, vanilla, and flour.
Pour into greased ramekins and bake for 12-14 minutes.
Serve immediately, with a scoop of ice cream if desired.

Chocolate Pudding
Ingredients:

- 2 cups milk
- 2 tbsp cornstarch
- ½ cup sugar
- ¼ cup cocoa powder
- 1 tsp vanilla extract

Instructions:
Whisk together cornstarch, sugar, cocoa, and milk in a saucepan.
Bring to a boil, whisking constantly, until thickened.
Remove from heat and stir in vanilla.
Chill in the fridge for at least 2 hours before serving.

Chocolate Tart

Ingredients:

- 1 ½ cups chocolate cookie crumbs (or crushed graham crackers)
- ¼ cup melted butter
- 12 oz dark chocolate
- 1 cup heavy cream
- 1 tsp vanilla extract

Instructions:
Preheat oven to 350°F (175°C).
Mix the cookie crumbs and melted butter, then press into a tart pan.
Bake the crust for 10 minutes, then let cool.
Heat the cream in a saucepan until it begins to simmer, then pour over chopped chocolate.
Stir until smooth and let cool slightly before pouring into the tart crust.
Refrigerate for at least 2 hours before serving.

Chocolate Cupcakes
Ingredients:

- 1 ¾ cups flour
- ½ cup cocoa powder
- 1 tsp baking soda
- 1 tsp baking powder
- ½ tsp salt
- 1 cup sugar
- 2 eggs
- ½ cup milk
- ½ cup vegetable oil
- 1 tsp vanilla extract
- 1 cup boiling water

Instructions:
Preheat oven to 350°F (175°C).
Mix dry ingredients in one bowl.
In another bowl, whisk together eggs, milk, oil, and vanilla.
Combine both mixtures and add boiling water (the batter will be thin).
Pour into cupcake liners and bake for 18-20 minutes.
Cool completely before frosting.

Chocolate Cheesecake
Ingredients:

- 1 ½ cups chocolate cookie crumbs
- 4 tbsp melted butter
- 3 cups cream cheese (softened)
- 1 cup sugar
- 4 large eggs
- 8 oz melted dark chocolate
- 1 tsp vanilla extract

Instructions:
Preheat oven to 325°F (163°C).
Mix cookie crumbs and melted butter, then press into the bottom of a springform pan.
Beat cream cheese and sugar together until smooth, then add eggs one at a time.
Stir in melted chocolate and vanilla.
Pour over crust and bake for 50-60 minutes, or until set.
Cool, then refrigerate for at least 4 hours before serving.

Chocolate Ganache
Ingredients:

- 8 oz dark chocolate (chopped)
- 1 cup heavy cream

Instructions:
Heat cream in a saucepan until it begins to simmer.
Pour over chopped chocolate and let sit for 5 minutes.
Stir until smooth and shiny.
Use immediately as a glaze, or chill to thicken for filling or frosting.

Chocolate Almond Bark

Ingredients:

- 12 oz dark chocolate
- ½ cup chopped almonds
- ¼ cup sea salt (optional)

Instructions:
Melt chocolate in a heatproof bowl over simmering water.
Stir in chopped almonds and spread the mixture onto a parchment-lined baking sheet.
Sprinkle with sea salt, if desired.
Refrigerate until set, then break into pieces.

Chocolate Ice Cream

Ingredients:

- 2 cups heavy cream
- 1 cup milk
- ¾ cup sugar
- ¾ cup cocoa powder
- 1 tsp vanilla extract
- 3 large egg yolks

Instructions:
Whisk together milk, cream, sugar, and cocoa powder in a saucepan.
Heat until warm but not boiling.
Whisk egg yolks in a separate bowl, then slowly add the warm milk mixture to temper the eggs.
Return to the saucepan and cook over low heat until thickened.
Cool, then churn in an ice cream maker according to the manufacturer's instructions.

Chocolate Chip Muffins
Ingredients:

- 1 ½ cups flour
- 1 tsp baking powder
- ½ tsp baking soda
- ½ tsp salt
- ½ cup sugar
- 1 egg
- ½ cup milk
- ¼ cup vegetable oil
- 1 tsp vanilla extract
- 1 cup chocolate chips

Instructions:
Preheat oven to 350°F (175°C).
Combine dry ingredients in one bowl.
Whisk together wet ingredients in another bowl.
Fold the wet ingredients into the dry, then stir in chocolate chips.
Scoop into muffin tins and bake for 18-20 minutes.

Chocolate Soufflé

Ingredients:

- 6 oz dark chocolate
- 3 tbsp butter
- ½ cup sugar
- 3 large eggs (separated)
- 1 tsp vanilla extract
- Pinch of salt

Instructions:
Preheat oven to 375°F (190°C).
Melt chocolate and butter in a heatproof bowl.
Whisk egg yolks, sugar, and vanilla into the chocolate mixture.
Whisk egg whites with a pinch of salt until stiff peaks form.
Fold the egg whites into the chocolate mixture, then pour into greased ramekins.
Bake for 15-20 minutes until puffed and slightly set.
Serve immediately.

Chocolate Covered Strawberries

Ingredients:

- 1 lb fresh strawberries (washed and dried)
- 8 oz dark or milk chocolate (chopped)
- 2 tbsp vegetable oil (optional for smoothness)

Instructions:
Melt chocolate in a heatproof bowl over simmering water or in the microwave.
If desired, add vegetable oil to the melted chocolate for extra smoothness.
Dip each strawberry into the chocolate, coating it fully or halfway.
Place on a parchment-lined tray and let cool until the chocolate hardens.
Refrigerate if needed to speed up the process.

Chocolate-Dipped Pretzels

Ingredients:

- 1 bag mini pretzels
- 8 oz chocolate chips (dark, milk, or white)
- Sprinkles or sea salt (optional)

Instructions:
Melt chocolate in a heatproof bowl over simmering water or microwave.
Dip pretzels into the melted chocolate, coating them halfway or completely.
Place dipped pretzels on a parchment-lined tray.
Sprinkle with sea salt or sprinkles if desired.
Let cool and harden in the fridge.

Chocolate Eclairs
 Ingredients:

- 1 sheet puff pastry (or homemade choux pastry)
- 8 oz dark chocolate
- 1 cup heavy cream
- 1 tbsp powdered sugar

Instructions:
Preheat oven to 400°F (200°C).
Bake puff pastry according to package instructions or make choux pastry.
While pastry is cooling, whip heavy cream with powdered sugar until stiff peaks form.
Melt chocolate and mix with a small amount of cream to create a glaze.
Fill cooled eclairs with whipped cream and dip the tops in the chocolate glaze.

Chocolate Hazelnut Spread
Ingredients:

- 1 ½ cups roasted hazelnuts
- ½ cup powdered sugar
- 2 tbsp cocoa powder
- ½ tsp vanilla extract
- ½ cup vegetable oil (or hazelnut oil)

Instructions:
Blend hazelnuts in a food processor until smooth.
Add powdered sugar, cocoa powder, and vanilla extract, blending again.
Gradually add oil to reach a creamy consistency.
Store in an airtight container at room temperature or in the fridge.

Chocolate Fondue

Ingredients:

- 8 oz dark or milk chocolate (chopped)
- ½ cup heavy cream
- 1 tsp vanilla extract
- Fruit, marshmallows, or biscuits for dipping

Instructions:
Heat cream in a saucepan until warm.
Add chopped chocolate and stir until smooth and melted.
Stir in vanilla extract.
Transfer to a fondue pot or serving bowl.
Serve with fruits, marshmallows, or biscuits for dipping.

Chocolate Milkshake
Ingredients:

- 2 cups vanilla ice cream
- 1 cup milk
- ¼ cup chocolate syrup
- Whipped cream and chocolate shavings (optional for garnish)

Instructions:
Blend ice cream, milk, and chocolate syrup until smooth.
Pour into glasses and top with whipped cream and chocolate shavings if desired.
Serve immediately.

Chocolate Chia Pudding
 Ingredients:

- 2 tbsp cocoa powder
- 3 tbsp chia seeds
- 1 cup almond milk (or regular milk)
- 2 tbsp honey or maple syrup

Instructions:
Whisk together cocoa powder, chia seeds, milk, and sweetener in a bowl.
Let sit in the fridge for at least 4 hours or overnight.
Stir before serving and top with fruit, granola, or nuts if desired.

Chocolate Peanut Butter Cups
Ingredients:

- 1 cup chocolate chips
- ½ cup peanut butter
- 2 tbsp powdered sugar
- ½ tsp vanilla extract

Instructions:
Melt half of the chocolate chips and pour into the bottom of muffin liners, then freeze for 10 minutes.
Mix peanut butter, powdered sugar, and vanilla extract until smooth.
Spoon a small amount of peanut butter mixture onto the set chocolate.
Top with the remaining melted chocolate and freeze until firm.

Hot Chocolate
Ingredients:

- 2 cups milk
- 2 tbsp cocoa powder
- 2 tbsp sugar (or to taste)
- ½ tsp vanilla extract
- Whipped cream or marshmallows (optional)

Instructions:
Heat milk in a saucepan over medium heat.
Whisk in cocoa powder and sugar until fully dissolved.
Remove from heat and stir in vanilla extract.
Pour into mugs and top with whipped cream or marshmallows if desired.

Chocolate Croissants
Ingredients:

- 1 sheet puff pastry
- 4 oz chocolate (dark, milk, or white), chopped
- 1 egg (for egg wash)

Instructions:
Preheat oven to 375°F (190°C).
Roll out the puff pastry and cut into squares.
Place a piece of chocolate in the center of each square.
Fold the pastry over to form a triangle and seal the edges.
Brush with beaten egg for a golden finish.
Bake for 15-20 minutes or until golden brown.

Chocolate Coconut Balls
Ingredients:

- 1 ½ cups shredded coconut
- 1 cup dark chocolate chips
- ¼ cup sweetened condensed milk
- 1 tsp vanilla extract

Instructions:
Melt the chocolate chips and condensed milk together in a heatproof bowl.
Mix in shredded coconut and vanilla extract.
Shape the mixture into small balls and chill in the fridge for about 30 minutes until firm.

Chocolate Popcorn

Ingredients:

- 1 bag microwave popcorn (or 6 cups air-popped)
- 1 cup dark chocolate chips
- 1 tbsp coconut oil (optional for smoother chocolate)
- Sea salt (optional)

Instructions:
Pop the popcorn and spread it on a baking sheet.
Melt the chocolate chips and coconut oil in a microwave or double boiler.
Drizzle the melted chocolate over the popcorn.
Sprinkle with sea salt if desired and let cool before serving.

Chocolate Banana Bread
Ingredients:

- 2 ripe bananas, mashed
- 1 cup sugar
- 2 eggs
- ½ cup melted butter
- 1 ½ cups flour
- 1 tsp baking soda
- ½ tsp salt
- 1 cup chocolate chips

Instructions:
Preheat oven to 350°F (175°C).
Mix mashed bananas, sugar, eggs, and melted butter in a bowl.
In another bowl, whisk together flour, baking soda, and salt.
Combine the dry and wet ingredients, then fold in the chocolate chips.
Pour into a greased loaf pan and bake for 60-65 minutes or until a toothpick comes out clean.

Chocolate Chip Pancakes
Ingredients:

- 1 cup flour
- 1 tbsp sugar
- 1 tsp baking powder
- ½ tsp baking soda
- ½ tsp salt
- 1 egg
- 1 cup buttermilk
- 2 tbsp melted butter
- ½ cup chocolate chips

Instructions:
Whisk together dry ingredients in one bowl.
In another bowl, whisk together egg, buttermilk, and melted butter.
Add wet ingredients to dry ingredients and stir until just combined.
Fold in chocolate chips.
Cook pancakes on a griddle over medium heat until bubbles form, then flip and cook the other side.

Chocolate Caramel Brownies

Ingredients:

- 1 box brownie mix (or homemade)
- ½ cup caramel sauce
- 1 cup chocolate chips

Instructions:
Prepare brownie mix according to package instructions.
Pour half of the brownie batter into a greased baking pan.
Drizzle with caramel sauce and sprinkle with chocolate chips.
Top with remaining brownie batter and bake according to the package instructions.

Chocolate Chip Scones
Ingredients:

- 2 cups flour
- 1/3 cup sugar
- 2 ½ tsp baking powder
- ¼ tsp salt
- 1 stick cold butter (cubed)
- ½ cup chocolate chips
- 1 egg
- 1 tsp vanilla extract
- ½ cup heavy cream

Instructions:
Preheat oven to 400°F (200°C).
Whisk dry ingredients in a bowl.
Cut in cold butter until mixture resembles coarse crumbs.
Stir in chocolate chips.
Whisk egg, vanilla, and cream together and add to the dry mixture.
Turn dough out onto a floured surface and gently knead.
Shape into a circle, cut into wedges, and bake for 15-20 minutes.

Chocolate-Orange Truffles
Ingredients:

- 8 oz dark chocolate
- ½ cup heavy cream
- 1 tsp orange zest
- 1 tbsp orange liqueur (optional)
- Cocoa powder or crushed nuts for coating

Instructions:
Heat cream in a saucepan until simmering.
Pour over chopped chocolate and let sit for a few minutes, then stir until smooth.
Stir in orange zest and liqueur.
Refrigerate for 2 hours until firm enough to shape.
Form into balls and roll in cocoa powder or crushed nuts.

Chocolate-Covered Almonds
Ingredients:

- 1 cup whole almonds
- 8 oz dark or milk chocolate (chopped)
- 1 tbsp coconut oil (optional for smoothness)

Instructions:
Melt chocolate and coconut oil (if using) in a heatproof bowl over simmering water or in the microwave.
Dip almonds into the melted chocolate, coating each one completely.
Place them on a parchment-lined tray and let cool until the chocolate hardens.
Refrigerate to speed up the process.

Chocolate Dipped Marshmallows

Ingredients:

- 1 package marshmallows
- 8 oz dark or milk chocolate (chopped)
- Sprinkles or crushed nuts (optional)

Instructions:

Melt chocolate in a heatproof bowl over simmering water or in the microwave.
Dip each marshmallow into the melted chocolate, coating it halfway or completely.
Sprinkle with crushed nuts or sprinkles if desired.
Place on a parchment-lined tray and let cool until set.

Chocolate Macarons
Ingredients:

- 1 cup powdered sugar
- 1 cup almond flour
- 3 large egg whites
- ¼ cup granulated sugar
- 2 tbsp cocoa powder
- 8 oz chocolate ganache (for filling)

Instructions:
Preheat oven to 300°F (150°C).
Sift together powdered sugar, almond flour, and cocoa powder.
Whisk egg whites until soft peaks form, then add granulated sugar and continue whisking until stiff peaks form.
Fold in the dry ingredients until smooth.
Pipe small rounds onto a baking sheet and let rest for 20-30 minutes.
Bake for 15-18 minutes and allow to cool completely.
Sandwich the macarons with chocolate ganache.

Chocolate-Covered Pretzel Bites

Ingredients:

- 1 bag mini pretzels
- 8 oz chocolate (dark, milk, or white)
- Sprinkles or crushed candy (optional)

Instructions:
Melt chocolate in a heatproof bowl over simmering water or in the microwave.
Dip each pretzel into the melted chocolate, coating it halfway.
Place on a parchment-lined tray and sprinkle with toppings if desired.
Let the chocolate harden before serving.

Chocolate Ricotta Pie
Ingredients:

- 2 cups ricotta cheese
- 1 cup dark chocolate chips
- ½ cup sugar
- 1 tsp vanilla extract
- 3 large eggs
- 1 pre-made pie crust

Instructions:
Preheat oven to 350°F (175°C).
Beat ricotta cheese, sugar, eggs, and vanilla together in a bowl until smooth.
Fold in chocolate chips.
Pour the mixture into the pie crust and bake for 40-45 minutes or until set.
Let cool before slicing and serving.

Chocolate Toffee Bars

Ingredients:

- 1 ½ cups graham cracker crumbs
- 1 cup butter (melted)
- 1 cup sugar
- 2 cups chocolate chips
- 1 cup chopped nuts (optional)

Instructions:
Preheat oven to 350°F (175°C).
Mix graham cracker crumbs, melted butter, and sugar together and press into a baking pan.
Bake for 10 minutes.
Top with chocolate chips and nuts, if using, and return to the oven for another 5 minutes, or until the chocolate is melted.
Spread the melted chocolate evenly and let cool before cutting into bars.

Chocolate Rice Krispies Treats
Ingredients:

- 6 cups Rice Krispies cereal
- 3 cups mini marshmallows
- 4 tbsp butter
- ½ cup chocolate chips (optional)

Instructions:
Melt butter in a large saucepan over low heat, then add marshmallows and stir until melted.
Remove from heat and fold in Rice Krispies cereal.
Press the mixture into a greased 9x13-inch pan.
Melt chocolate chips and drizzle over the treats, then let cool before cutting into squares.

Chocolate Tiramisu
Ingredients:

- 1 package ladyfinger cookies
- 1 ½ cups strong brewed coffee (cooled)
- 1 ½ cups mascarpone cheese
- 1 cup heavy cream
- ¼ cup powdered sugar
- 2 oz dark chocolate (grated)
- 2 tbsp cocoa powder

Instructions:
Dip ladyfingers into the cooled coffee and layer them at the bottom of a dish.
Beat mascarpone cheese, heavy cream, and powdered sugar together until smooth.
Spread half of the mascarpone mixture over the ladyfingers.
Add another layer of dipped ladyfingers and the rest of the mascarpone mixture.
Top with grated chocolate and dust with cocoa powder.
Chill in the refrigerator for at least 4 hours before serving.

Chocolate Coconut Macaroons

Ingredients:

- 2 ½ cups sweetened shredded coconut
- 2/3 cup egg whites (about 4 eggs)
- ½ cup sugar
- 1 tsp vanilla extract
- 8 oz dark or milk chocolate (for dipping)

Instructions:

Preheat the oven to 325°F (165°C).
Whisk egg whites until soft peaks form, then add sugar and vanilla, continuing to whisk until stiff peaks form.
Fold in shredded coconut.
Scoop tablespoon-sized portions onto a parchment-lined baking sheet.
Bake for 18-20 minutes, or until golden.
Cool completely, then dip the bottoms of each macaroon into melted chocolate. Let set.

Chocolate Cherry Cake

Ingredients:

- 1 cup all-purpose flour
- 1/2 cup cocoa powder
- 1 ½ tsp baking powder
- 1/2 tsp baking soda
- 1/2 tsp salt
- 1 cup sugar
- 2 large eggs
- 1/2 cup milk
- 1/4 cup vegetable oil
- 1 tsp vanilla extract
- 1 cup maraschino cherries, chopped
- 1 cup dark chocolate chips

Instructions:
Preheat oven to 350°F (175°C).
Mix dry ingredients (flour, cocoa, baking powder, baking soda, salt) in a bowl.
In another bowl, beat eggs, sugar, milk, oil, and vanilla.
Add dry ingredients to wet and stir until combined.
Fold in chopped cherries and chocolate chips.
Pour the batter into a greased cake pan and bake for 30-35 minutes or until a toothpick comes out clean.

Chocolate Ice Cream Sandwiches

Ingredients:

- 1 package chocolate chip cookies (store-bought or homemade)
- 1 pint vanilla or chocolate ice cream

Instructions:

Scoop a generous amount of ice cream onto one cookie.
Top with another cookie to create a sandwich.
Freeze for at least 2 hours before serving.
Enjoy cold and creamy!

Chocolate Chip Cheesecake Bars
Ingredients:

- 1 ½ cups graham cracker crumbs
- ¼ cup sugar
- 6 tbsp butter (melted)
- 2 cups cream cheese (softened)
- 1 cup sugar
- 2 eggs
- 1 tsp vanilla extract
- 1 ½ cups chocolate chips

Instructions:
Preheat oven to 325°F (165°C).
Mix graham cracker crumbs, sugar, and melted butter, and press into the bottom of a greased 9x13-inch pan.
In a separate bowl, beat cream cheese and sugar until smooth.
Add eggs and vanilla, and beat until combined.
Pour over the crust and sprinkle with chocolate chips.
Bake for 30-35 minutes, until set. Cool completely and refrigerate before cutting into bars.

Chocolate-Dipped Biscotti
Ingredients:

- 1 ½ cups all-purpose flour
- 1 cup sugar
- 1 tsp baking powder
- ¼ tsp salt
- 2 large eggs
- 1 tsp vanilla extract
- 1 cup dark chocolate (for dipping)

Instructions:
Preheat oven to 350°F (175°C).
Mix flour, sugar, baking powder, and salt in a bowl.
Whisk eggs and vanilla, and add to the dry ingredients.
Shape the dough into a log and place on a greased baking sheet.
Bake for 25-30 minutes, then remove and cool for 10 minutes.
Slice into biscotti, return to the oven, and bake for 10-15 more minutes.
Once cooled, dip the ends in melted chocolate and let set.

Chocolate Peanut Butter Brownies

Ingredients:

- 1 box brownie mix (or homemade)
- ½ cup peanut butter
- ¼ cup powdered sugar
- ¼ cup chocolate chips

Instructions:

Prepare brownie mix according to instructions and bake.

Mix peanut butter and powdered sugar until smooth, then swirl it into the batter halfway through baking.

Top with chocolate chips during the last 5 minutes of baking, letting them melt into the brownies.

Chocolate Fudge Cake
Ingredients:

- 1 ½ cups flour
- 1 cup cocoa powder
- 1 ½ cups sugar
- 1 tsp baking powder
- 1 tsp baking soda
- ½ tsp salt
- 2 large eggs
- 1 cup buttermilk
- ½ cup vegetable oil
- 1 tsp vanilla extract
- 1 cup boiling water

Instructions:
Preheat oven to 350°F (175°C).
Mix all dry ingredients together.
In a separate bowl, beat the eggs, buttermilk, oil, and vanilla.
Combine wet and dry ingredients, then add boiling water (batter will be thin).
Pour into greased pans and bake for 30-35 minutes.
Cool and frost with chocolate ganache or icing.

Chocolate Mint Cookies
Ingredients:

- 1 ½ cups flour
- ½ cup cocoa powder
- 1 tsp baking soda
- ¼ tsp salt
- 1 cup unsalted butter
- 1 ½ cups sugar
- 1 large egg
- 2 tsp peppermint extract
- 1 cup chocolate chips (optional)

Instructions:
Preheat oven to 350°F (175°C).
In a bowl, whisk together flour, cocoa powder, baking soda, and salt.
In another bowl, beat butter and sugar until smooth, then add egg and peppermint extract.
Fold in the dry ingredients and chocolate chips if using.
Scoop dough onto baking sheets and bake for 10-12 minutes. Let cool.

Chocolate Cinnamon Rolls

Ingredients:

- 1 package cinnamon roll dough (or homemade)
- ½ cup cocoa powder
- 1 cup chocolate chips
- ½ cup sugar
- 2 tbsp butter (melted)

Instructions:

Roll out cinnamon roll dough and spread melted butter on top.
Sprinkle with cocoa powder, sugar, and chocolate chips.
Roll up the dough and slice into rolls.
Place the rolls in a baking dish and bake according to package directions.
Top with icing and enjoy!